TOMMY TORQUIL

WALKING

The Ultimate Guide to Starting a Walking Routine for Beginners, Discover All the Information You Need to Know to Start Walking For Fitness and Greater Overall Health

Descrierea CIP a Bibliotecii Naţionale a României
TOMMY TORQUIL
   WALKING. The Ultimate Guide to Starting a Walking Routine for Beginners, Discover All the Information You Need to Know to Start Walking For Fitness and Greater Overall Health / Tommy Torquil – Bucharest: Editura My Ebook, 2020
   ISBN

TOMMY TORQUIL

WALKING

The Ultimate Guide to Starting a Walking Routine for Beginners, Discover All the Information You Need to Know to Start Walking For Fitness and Greater Overall Health

My Ebook Publishing House
Bucharest, 2020

TOMMY TORONTO

There are so many reasons walking is good for you, it's virtually impossible to talk about all of them in one short report. So, think of this as a mini primer. Before we get into the "why" of things, here are some fun and interesting facts about walking:

- Every step you take uses up to 200 muscles.
- The average person walks the equivalent distance of five equators in his or her lifetime.
- Believe it or not, it's better to swing your arms when you walk. Why? When you don't, it increases the effort of walking up to 12 percent.
- Under certain circumstances, when you walk, the pressure you put on your feet exceeds your total body weight. If you run, this pressure can be up to three or four times your weight.
- Want to burn more calories? Try walking sideways. It actually gets rid of 78 percent more of the little culprits.
- Walking uphill increases cardiovascular fitness and muscle tone.
- It takes approximately one hour 43 minutes to walk off 540 calories, which happens to be the caloric count of a Big Mac. If your meal included a super-size Coke and

French fries, you need to walk seven hours to burn the calories.

- If you're trying to improve your health, experts suggest walking 6,000 steps per day. If you're trying to lose weight, walk a total of 10,000 steps to get the job done.
- Some people get exercise via walking, even when they don't want to. Sleepwalking, also known as somnambulism, affects approximately 18 percent of the world's population.
- The term "walk" comes from the old English word "wealcan," which means "to roll."
- It's extremely important to be constantly aware of your surroundings when you walk. Statistics indicate a person is 36 more times likely to be killed walking than driving a car and 300 times more likely to be killed walking than traveling via airplane.

Now it's time to cover some of the many reasons walking is good for you and an excellent way to keep fit. One of the greatest things about walking is the fact that you benefit from it, no matter how much or how little you walk. Of course, the more you walk the better. But, every little bit helps.

THE BENEFITS OF WALKING

Walking every day is one of the easiest and healthiest things you can do for your body. It costs nothing to take a walk. You can do it anywhere, during any season and in any weather. Not only do you reap the benefits of being outdoors taking in fresh air and sunshine, if you choose to walk outdoors, but the benefits of walking in any location are far and wide.

Heart Health

Studies show that walking regularly lowers your risk of both heart disease and stroke. Walking gets your heart rate up and causes your body to burn calories. This, in turn, lowers your cholesterol level.

According to The Stroke Association, walking for half an hour every day helps to keep your blood pressure in check and reduces your risk of stroke by up to 27 percent. Walking gives your circulation a boost and helps to increase the levels of oxygen in your blood. This actually leads to feeling more energetic after a short (brisk) walk.

Walking isn't going to build muscle as effectively as other more strenuous exercises. However, a walking routine does help you burn fat and build some muscle, especially in the legs. Walking gives your calves and your thighs quite a workout. It also helps your glutes.

Compared to more high-impact exercises such as running, walking is also very gentle on people with arthritis. It's relatively easy to choose a route, head outside and give your muscles the workout they need.

Weight Loss

According to Mayo Clinic, walking isn't the best way to lose weight. But it certainly helps. To lose one pound per week, consider eliminating roughly 500 calories from your diet each day.

Walking is actually of more importance after you lose weight. Studies indicate the people who are most successful keeping weight off are those who participate in frequent physical activities. One of the most important things to remember is balance. Overdoing any form of exercise is dangerous. Start slow and gradually build up to a longer regimen.

After 30 minutes of walking at about 2 mph, you'll have burned around 75 calories. If you manage to get your speed up to around 3 mph, the number goes up to approximately 100 calories. While a single hour of walking may not burn an impressive amount of calories (around as much as, say, a glass of chocolate milk would give you), these numbers add up when you work walking into your routine.

Improved Immune System

According to some studies, walking regularly benefits your immune system. Exercise such as walking causes our body to produce increased levels of several types of critical immune cells. Exposure to the sun also boosts our levels of vitamin D, which improves the performance of our immune systems as well as bone health.

Brain Booster

While you may not think it's true, walking is also good for your brain. Walking has been shown to have multiple cognitive benefits, including improved cognitive control, improved academic performance and a boost of creativity in young people.

10

This boost in creativity is especially prominent when young people walk outdoors, as exposure to a natural setting is thought to stimulate creativity.

Seniors who walk regularly are also shown to have improved memory function. The farther an elderly person can walk in a six-minute span of time, the better they tend to perform on memory and logic tests. Studies also show that elderly people who walk over six miles a week are less likely to experience brain shrinkage and dementia as the years go by.

Not only is walking good for your brain, it's also good for your mood. Studies show that even moderate exercise such as a brisk walk causes our body to release endorphins - the neurotransmitter found in our brains that causes us to feel happiness and euphoria.

Walking regularly can stave off the negative effects of anxiety or stress. Establishing and sticking to a walking routine also gives you a sense of setting and completing goals, which can raise your self-esteem and leave you feeling more confident in yourself. What better reason to walk in a relaxing or a natural environment?

Another reason walking is great for your mood is it gives you time to think. Walking doesn't take that much effort, so while we do it, we can ponder other areas in our lives. This gives you a chance to work through your problems in a relatively quiet and safe environment.

After starting a walking routine, you may find that you have your best ideas while walking around your neighborhood or down a trail through the forest. For some, walking is even similar to medication. The simple repetitive activity allows you to get out your anxiety while allowing your mind to tune out.

WALKING WHILE PREGNANT

More and more moms-to-be are realizing and taking advantage of the benefits of walking while pregnant. If you're expecting and have yet to take up walking, now is the perfect time to do so. Here are a few reasons why:

- Walking lowers the risk of pre-eclampsia. Since it helps to reduce your cholesterol, in a somewhat roundabout way, and helps maintain your weight, your chances of dealing with high blood pressure are much lower.

- It lowers the risk of gestational diabetes. Again, because walking helps you maintain your weight when pregnant, you have much less chance of getting this temporary form of diabetes.

- Your chances of having a healthy baby are higher. When you stay at the optimum pregnancy weight, it typically means your baby is also maintaining a healthy weight. If you're worried about delivering a heavy baby, you might consider walking to reduce the chances of weight being a delivery-related issue.

- Because walking strengthens your muscles and increases your flexibility, women who walk during pregnancy typically have an easier time with childbirth. This can mean less pain in a much faster delivery time.

Almost everyone knows that pregnancy causes at least some level of stress. For some women, this level is much higher than others. In addition, hormones cause moods to go from extreme happiness one minute to downright depression the next.

As mentioned above, when you walk your body releases endorphins. Endorphins are magical in a sense, because they make you feel good. So, even if your schedule only allows infrequent walks when pregnant, take advantage of each and every one of them.

Taking the steps instead of the elevator, grocery shopping, trying to walk just a little more at work or getting off the bus one stop early are all ways to add extra walking to your daily routine.

There are a couple of special safety precautions to keep in mind as a pregnant walker. Don't let your body get too overheated. Doing so can sometimes lead to premature labor. If it's warm outside, consider walking in the mall. In addition, because of your large belly, your center of gravity has shifted. Because of this, you always want to walk with extra caution.

When you're pregnant, you probably don't want to go into "power walker mode," unless walking was part of your daily routine before you got pregnant. Never walk too fast. It's best to walk at a comfortable pace. Try to remember to take a few sips of water every five minutes or so. You don't want to get dehydrated. It's bad for you and the baby!

Getting the Right Shoes

When it comes to walking shoes, no single pair is going to be a good fit for everybody. The most important thing to keep in mind is comfort. Make sure that walking right in your shoes feels comfortable and that the shoes fit properly. Try to leave about 1/2 inch between the tip of your toes and the end of the shoe. Here a few more things to keep in mind as you select your hiking footwear:

- Try to find a shoe that is both lightweight and breathable. Thicker, heavier shoes will be less comfortable both to walk in and to wear for extended periods of time.

16

- Having a supportive heel is much better than a thick one. A shoe with a thicker heel causes your foot to slap down all at once rather than roll naturally.

- Make sure that you find a shoe with a sole that bends easily at the ball of the foot. Your foot needs to be able to lead with your heel, then roll to the ball of your foot. A thick sole will always get in the way of this.

- Go shopping for your new shoes in the evening. Why? After walking around all day, your feet may be a little swollen. You want to be sure your shoes fit comfortably after being on your feet all day, and this is the best way to do it. Also, make sure you aren't in a rush when deciding on walking shoes. You really need to take the time to walk around the store, to get an initial feel for the fit.

- After you pick out your new shoes, wear them around the house for a few days to break them in. The last thing you want to do is limp home the first time you "officially" go walking in them. This way, if anything about the shoes doesn't agree with you, you'll be able to take them back before they get all scuffed up outside.

- If you can, keep track of the number of miles that you walk while wearing your shoes. As a general guideline, it may be best to replace them every 250 to 500 miles. Of course, if they become damaged or worn out before then, be sure to replace them rather than wear them while damaged.

OTHER NECESSARY EQUIPMENT

Clothing

When it comes to walking outdoors, the best clothes to wear varies greatly depending on the location and climate. It's generally best to avoid darker colors, because they absorb the heat of sunlight. If you'll be walking near a road or street, consider wearing a reflective vest or patches to ensure that drivers of passing cars will see you when it gets dark.

While cotton is a very common material, it may not be the best choice for hiking clothes. When cotton gets wet, it becomes a poor insulator and is not good at trapping body heat. This means you'll feel much colder and face a higher risk of hypothermia. Instead, try to find clothing made of wool or synthetic materials.

Don't forget to look for the right socks when you put your hiking outfit together. Socks that are made for hiking tend to provide more cushioning than typical cotton tube socks. They also tend to breathe better, which cuts down on sweat and leaves you more comfortable during long walks.

Waterproof

Even when the weather is nice, it's a good idea to wear a waterproof, windproof jacket. You never know when conditions are going to take a turn, and a good windbreaker goes a long way toward keeping you dry and comfortable. If rain is a possibility on the day of your hike, you might also consider carrying a rain poncho.

During wet weather, wearing hiking pants is a good way to keep your legs dry when you walk. These pants tend to be more durable than slacks or jeans, as well as more water resistant. Hiking or rain pants protect you from rain, puddles and any mud or brush you may encounter on your favorite nature trail.

Thermal

Cold weather can make a long hike much less pleasurable. The best way to keep warm during a hike is to wear insulated or thermal clothing that keeps your body heat in and the cold out. A wool sweater is a good choice because it is well insulated and more water resistant than a cotton shirt. In particularly cold weather, thermal underwear is great for staying warm, although harder to take off than a sweater, should the weather take a turn for the better.

Backpack and Bags

Whether you're hiking down trails or through an urban setting, you need something to carry all your gear in. If you don't plan to take much with you, a smaller belt pouch or messenger bag will usually do the trick. But, if you're planning a longer hike, it's best to carry a backpack. While a school-style book bag holds plenty of supplies, a hiking bag is the recommended choice. Among other things, it's designed with better storage capabilities and added comfort in mind.

Even if your bag doesn't seem too heavy at first, carrying it for prolonged periods can really wear out your back, arms and shoulders. If you're walking with a heavy load, make sure you take frequent breaks to give your shoulders a rest. If you're carrying a messenger bag that only goes over one shoulder, switch sides frequently so that both sides of your body share the burden.

GPS and Navigation

In this day and age, many people already carry a GPS with them at all times. Even a basic navigation app, such as Google Maps, can be indispensable - both walking around the neighborhood and through the woods. Provided your cell phone has service, determining the best path to your destination can be as simple as a single tap. However, for routes that take you deep into nature, it may be best to travel with an actual GPS. A device designed for hiking typically has a much longer battery life than most smartphones, especially if you use your phone to play music on the trail.

Not only can a smartphone act as a guide with the proper GPS app, many other apps also offer other useful services to hikers. MapMyWalk serves as a GPS, calorie counter and route planner, all in one. In addition to tracking your progress on each walk, MapMyWalk stores data from hikes you've taken in the past in order to let you see a clear picture of your fitness progress.

Not only can you save data from previous walks, you can also share the information with your walking-enthusiast friends (to compare everyone's progress) and post achievement notifications on your favorite social media sites. This brings a social aspect to your walks without the need to locate a walking group in your area.

Of course, MapMyWalk isn't the only app out there that's useful to fitness junkies. There are countless pedometer apps available as a free download, many of which offer unique designs or features. Not only that, services like Google Fit or Samsung's S Health provide a free way to plan and track your fitness journey. No matter which path you choose to explore, the use of an additional tool to track your progress is a great motivator that will no doubt keep you walking for years to come.

Food and Drink

Whenever you go out for a walk, be sure to bring plenty of water with you. If you don't stay hydrated, you can end up suffering from the effects of fatigue or even heat exhaustion. While any water bottle will do, there is a variety of bottles designed with hiking in mind that are durable and lightweight. If you're planning a trip that's going to last more than a day, it's probably a good idea to pack a water filter or water purification tablets too.

As far as food goes, you want to pack non-perishables that won't weigh you down. This is especially true with longer walking excursions. Experienced hikers recommend eating lots of carbohydrates and proteins, which provide fast energy and keeps muscles healthy. Dehydrated foods are ideal, because they are easier to carry. Many walkers dehydrate and package their own trail snacks at home. It's a much cheaper alternative to store-bought brands. It also greatly reduces packaging waste.

Remember, what you bring along with you can vary greatly from one walk to the next. If you're taking a walk through your neighborhood, you won't need much more than a good pair of shoes and a bottle of water. But, it doesn't hurt to think about the addition of walking-related accessories. Choose from a variety of different fitness tools to help you get the most out of your walking workout. For example, weights and resistance bands are popular choices. Both are user-friendly and won't break the bank.

FOR YOUR SAFETY

If you live in an urban or suburban area, your best bet for a free walking route is likely the sidewalk or shoulder along the streets of your town. It's crucial when walking near traffic to always be aware of your surroundings.

If there's sidewalk available along your route, make it your first choice. Only walk along the shoulder of the road when there is no other alternative. If you must travel along the shoulder, make sure you walk facing traffic. That way, you can see cars approaching you and have time to react should any of the drivers not be paying attention.

Make sure you apply sunscreen before you set out on your journey, and bring extra along in case you need to reapply it. It doesn't take long for sunburn to develop. You'll definitely regret it the next day if it does.

Believe it or not, even on a cloudy day, as much as 80 percent of the sun's UV radiation makes it through our atmosphere. That being said, look for a sport sunscreen, or at least one that's sweat resistant. Pay close attention to how often the label indicates you need to apply the product and follow the instructions to a tee.

Stinging or biting insects are a common problem along the trails, especially in the seasons that bring on great hiking weather. The best way to keep the bugs at bay is to use insect repellent, whether it's an aerosol spray or lotion. It's important to bring along enough insect repellent for everybody, especially if you'll still be hiking at dusk.

Texting Dangers

Years ago, before the age of texting, walking wasn't quite as dangerous. Today, thousands of pedestrians are treated in local emergency rooms as a result of texting at the wrong time. What's more disturbing is the fact that these numbers might even be higher. Why? Many people are too embarrassed to admit they fell or injured themselves in some other manner, while texting and walking.

Using your phone while you walk is more distracting than you might think. You're doing something else, looking at something else and your mind is somewhere else. Think of it as three strikes against you.

A recent study conducted by Stony Brook University indicates that an individual using a phone and walking at the same time is 61 percent more likely to veer off course. Yes, you read that right - a whopping 61 percent.

In a separate University at Buffalo study, data supports the fact that more pedestrians are injured (per mile) using cell phones than riding in vehicles. When you think about it, those facts are really quite frightening.

Make a concerted effort to ignore your cell phone when walking. Take it with you in the event of an emergency. But, as a rule, you'll be much safer if you just enjoy your surroundings and "just say no" to texting. You can always take up where you left off once you return home.

One last word of caution: the longer your proposed walking or hiking route, the more effort you probably want to put into the planning stages.

TRACKING YOUR PROGRESS

When you're walking for the sake of fitness, it's important to keep track of when and how far you walk. If you don't keep track of your progress, it can be difficult to plan out an effective walking schedule for the future. One of the best tools you can use to keep track of your walks is a walking journal or a calendar. With either (or even both) of these, you can easily take note of how far you walk every day.

Another useful walking tool is a pedometer, which keeps track of how many steps you take. This lets you keep a more accurate measure of how much you work out than tracking the time or distance that you walk. There are a wide variety of pedometers available on the market, as well as apps that let your smartphone track your steps.

Sticking to Your Walking Routine

Once you start following the routine you've established, it can be easy to slack off if you're not careful. If you let yourself slip or decide to "take it easy" for a day, it can eventually lead to you dropping the walking routine altogether. Here are a couple of ways you can keep your walking routine engaging and fun.

Set Goals

Establishing goals for yourself is a sure way to get the most out of any activity. Goals help you to structure your time and effort. They also give you something to work toward, which provides you with reason to push yourself. Achieving your goals also makes you feel accomplished, which leads to a boost to your self-esteem.

Setting goals is especially important when it comes to walking for fitness. Of course, walking is still great for your body if you set out without a plan. You will still get some benefit out of each walk. However, in order for walking to have a serious positive impact on your health, you'll have to walk on a more regular basis.

It's best to start out small. For many new walkers, this means planning to walk for around fifteen to twenty minutes. While this may not seem like much walking, remember that it's important to set goals that aren't too hard to accomplish. If, once you go on your walk, twenty minutes doesn't seem like enough, feel free to start out with a longer walk next time.

Once you have determined a reasonable distance goal, and you've managed to achieve it with each of your walks, it's important to step it up. Of course, how exactly you add to your workout is up to you. But, if you add some time to each workout at regular intervals, you can expand on the fitness progress you're already making.

Once your goals are established, backing down from your walking routine will be like breaking a promise to yourself. Keep track of how many days you can successfully follow your routine. This will give you that extra drive to get out and walk. If you're thinking about skipping a day, you'll have to reset your count.

Mix It Up

One reason you may find yourself straying from your walking routine is that doing the same thing day after day can become tedious. While this is true, there's no reason that your walk has to be the same every day. Turning each walk into a different experience can be as easy as walking in a different direction.

Walking in a new environment helps to keep walking fresh, even if you do it daily. This doesn't mean that you have to travel far away in order to walk. If you plan on walking around your neighborhood, use a street map to plan out several different routes of the same length.

Make Walking Fun

Consider one, two or all three of the following ideas to make walking fun. The first one is utilizing a free app such as Charity Miles, to help others. This app keeps track of the distance you walk and donates 25 cents per mile to one of several charities. Charities include Autism Speaks, Habitat for Humanity and Pencils of Promise. Obviously, the more you walk, the more the charity benefits.

Geocaching has been around for quite some time. In the event you've never heard of it, think of it as a high-tech treasure hunt of sorts. In simple terms, you pick a local geocache that sounds like something you'd love to find, and use any

GPS-enabled device (think cell phone) to locate it. You can easily download the official app and learn all about it at geocaching.com.

Invite a friend to join you for a movie or an afternoon of shopping. If you live within walking distance, getting there is a no-brainer. If your destination is too far away to walk to it, drive part of the way, park somewhere and walk the rest of the way. If you're shopping, think of the money you'll save because you won't want to be weighed down with shopping bags on your way back to your vehicle.

POWER WALKING

Once you've found your walking groove, you may want to kick things up a notch by adding "power walking" to your routine. Also referred to as "fitness walking" or even "race walking," power walking burns almost the same amount of calories as running. Even better, it's much easier on the body. The reason being, walking faster requires the use of more muscles. This, in turn, burns calories more quickly.

Once they get used to it, most fitness walkers are able to cover the distance of one mile in 13 to 15 minutes. Avoiding these common mistakes helps anyone to walk faster.

- Don't hunch your shoulders
- Don't use weights of any kind - this includes both ankle weights and hand weights
- Avoid looking at the ground
- Avoid over-striding

- Don't use excessive or vigorous arm movements

When you power walk, keep your shoulders down and relaxed possible. Use good posture, keeping your chin up to a high level. Try to look approximately 20 feet ahead of you. Take smaller steps. To make it easier, pretend you're walking along a straight line. Push off using your toes. Try to land on your heels. Breathe naturally, taking deep breaths. This helps you to get the most oxygen traveling through your system.

Your feet are always in contact with the ground when power walking. The good thing about this is the fact your body is never floating in mid-air, waiting to make harsh contact with the pavement with every step.

Statistics show powers walkers lose approximately four times as much total body fat as "regular speed" walkers, over the same period of time. Power walking, at four to five mph, burns close to 565 calories in 60 minutes.

Here is another interesting statistic. Women who participate in three 30-minute (high-intensity) walks and two normally-paced walks a week lose six times more belly fat than women who take five leisurely walks a week. Yes, six times! That's really something to think about.

Race-walking is basically a step up from power walking. There's actually a specific technique to it, as well as a strict set of rules. It is somewhat tricky to learn, but the benefits are greater. Race walkers get a much better cardio workout and burn more calories than other categories of walkers.

Getting Started

When it comes to walking to get or stay fit, this information is really just the beginning. If you're not yet convinced walking is for you, why not try walking on a "trial basis"? One-fourth of an average city block is equal to 200 steps. So, walking around the block, one time, racks up 800 steps. If that's too much to start out with, cut that distance in half and then challenge yourself to walk a little further each day.

If you don't want to walk alone, chances are a friend or family member will be willing to accompany you. Not only will you both benefit from the exercise, it's also a great way to catch up on gossip or just life in general after a hectic day. Not to mention there's safety in numbers.

Remember, walking as a wonderful family activity. Getting everyone involved is probably easier than you think. It's the perfect time to spend quality time together. In addition, it's never too early to start thinking about good health. You can almost guarantee that if they start exercising early, your kids will thank you for getting them involved when they get older.

Honestly, there's absolutely no better time than now to dust off your walking shoes and hit the trail, sidewalk or even your driveway. Everyone has to start somewhere. You won't know if you find it enjoyable until you try.

Printed by Libri Plureos GmbH in Hamburg,
Germany